Between sea

to Katie

Sandra Burnett

Between sea and sky

© Copyright Sandra Burnett 2019

Published by Half Moon Books 2019
An imprint of OWF Press Community Interest Company
Otley Courthouse, Courthouse Street
Otley, West Yorkshire LS21 3AN

www.owfpress.com

All rights reserved. No part of this book may be copied, reproduced, stored in a retrieval system or transmitted, in any form or by any electronic or mechanical means without the prior permission of the copyright owner.

Cover photo: © Pauline Sturges
Cover design by Nick Palmer

ISBN 978-1-9161668-0-6

Printed and bound by ImprintDigital.com, UK

Contents

Acknowledgements
Part I – Outside the frame
At Phillies ... 3
At the Square and Compass ... 4
The Artist in Her Studio ... 5
Mother Goddess ... 6
Gas 1940 ... 7
Port Vendres – La Ville c.1925 ... 8
Dancing to forget ... 9
Sea to sky ... 10
Part II – Once upon a time
Queen Zenobia ... 13
The daughter's story ... 17
Sirens ... 18
On Orchard Street ... 19
Conspiracies ... 20
Museum pieces ... 21
High tea ... 22
Moon myths ... 23
Last ... 24
Tidy sum ... 25
Part III – Ghosts
Hauntings ... 29
Between 7.30 and 8 a.m. ... 30
Shed ... 31
These foolish things ... 32
Navigating St George's Channel ... 33
The art of frying eggs ... 34
Part IV – Shades of childhood
Impact ... 37
Guardian ... 38
Being but kids ... 39
Arguments ... 40
Shrove Tuesday ... 41
Prey ... 42

Part V – Spotlight

sixties usherette	45
Last words	46
We all have the makings of a star	47
For the record	48
It's lunchtime and I've been reading Frank O'Hara	50

Part VI – Some you lose

Pre-nuptial	55
Note to silence	56
This is just to say	57
Blues Café	58
Saying it with flowers	59
Dandelion	60
Dreams	61
Swan song	62
Dance of doves at Lanzarote	63
The mistress	64

Part VII – To be continued

Leaving Palmyra – March 2011	67
Adrift	68
Mayday	69
Fighter	70
Invisible injuries	71
Some say	72
Good dog	73
On my last trip	74
The next Big Bang	75

Acknowledgements

Versions of the following poems have been credited in competitions or been published as follows:

'At the Square and Compass' in *Half Moon, Poems about Pubs* (Half Moon Books, 2016)

'Gas 1940' Highly Commended in NAWE competition *Provocations,* 2013

'Dancing to forget' in *Coast to Coast to Coast,* winter 2018/19

'Sea to sky' included in the *Leeds Lieder Festival, Poetry into Song,* 2018

'Sirens' in *New Lease* (Half Moon Books, 2016) and *Algebra of Owls Quarterly Anthology Number 2* and e-zine, 2016

'Moon Myths' in *Pale Fire – New Writings on the Moon* (Frogmore Press, 2019)

'Last' Highly Commended in *The Red Shed Poetry Competition 2017* and published in *The Quality of the Moment* (Currock Press, 2017)

'Tidy Sum' in *Whirlagust* (Yaffle Press, 2019)

'Navigating St George's Channel' published under the title 'Night Passage' in *Coast to Coast to Coast,* spring 2018

'Some say' joint 3rd in *Leeds Writers Circle Poetry Competition 2010*, and published in *Workout* (White Line Press for Poetry Gym, 2011) and *WordClub – 100 Thousand Poets for Change,* (e-zine, 2018)

'sixties usherette' in *Magma 71, The Film Issue,* 2018

'Last words' commended in *East Yorkshire Poetry Competition 2019* and published online

'For the record' 3rd prize in *Poems Please Me* competition 2015, and published in *New Lease* (Half Moon Books, 2016)

'It's lunchtime and I've been reading Frank O'Hara' in *Wolverhampton Literature Festival 2019, Poetry Anthology* (Write Out Loud)

'Note to Silence' Highly Commended, *Leeds Writers Circle Poetry Competition 2019*

'Saying it with flowers' in *Courthouse Writers – A Mixed Bunch, The Flowers of the Washburn* (Courthouse Writers, 2012)

'Dandelion' in *Courthouse Writers – A Mixed Bunch, Flowers of the Washburn* (Courthouse Writers, 2012)

and *The Garden: Poems that will Grow on You* (Half Moon Books, 2014)

'Mayday' *Leeds Writers Circle Poetry Plate,* 2018

'Fighter' in *Strix #5,* 2018

'Good Dog' *Leeds Writers Circle Poetry Plate,* 2017

'The next Big Bang' Commended in *The Otley Poetry Prize 2017* and published in *Strix #1,* 2017

My sincere thanks to Courthouse Writers, Otley Poetry Gym and Otley Stanza for helpful feedback; to Char March for thoughtful suggestions, encouragement and support in putting this collection together; to Pauline Sturges for the perfect cover photograph and to all at Half Moon Books – particularly Jane Kite, Roz Fairclough and Peter White (for his endless patience and care).

'One day I will find the right words, and they will be simple.' Jack Kerouac

Part I – Outside the frame

At Phillies
(after Nighthawks by Edward Hopper, 1942)

I see a woman in red. She does not wish to drink alone.
Her companion, a stranger in town, misses his wife.
They hold the bartender's attention.

The man with his back to me is down to his last dollar.
He studies his watch. For me it has to be engraved,
For 30 years loyal service.

The bartender has a girl; for now she's not part
of the composition but will be back, scruffy
and skint and blubbering excuses.

This quartet owns the night. They take no questions.
They take no advice. I keep my distance so as not
to inhale a germ of their pain.

And I want dawn to come – with its sniff of promise –
to make the bartender sneeze, and the woman in red
bless him as she leaves.

At the Square and Compass

There is a large mirror behind the bar,
so even with her back to the double doors,
buffing optics, she sees the biker enter
and turns to face him, square on,
sullen.

I'm reminded of a favourite painting,
whip out my phone.

When the pub empties I show her the photo.
I start to tell her about Manet's masterpiece.
She shuts me up, demands I delete because
she's no wish to be trapped with her ex
in the gallery on my SIM.

I erase the image with a pang of regret for the woman,
marooned since 1882, in *A Bar at the Folies-Bergère*.

The Artist in Her Studio
(after the painting by Paula Rego in Leeds Art Gallery)

You are invited in but be warned,
for there will be smoking and the scent of cabbage.

There are no kings or sealing wax,
but steel caps hide in brogues and your failure
to pull your gaze from the breasts of the nude
will prompt a kick.

The petite but stern-mouthed assistant
has summed you up for a dreamer,
not handsome enough to be model or muse
and too credulous for an agent.

Comments on half-completed works,
attempts to fiddle with the banjo-plucking monkey
or fondle the ears of the papier-mâché horse-head
are unwelcome.

Stand back to notice how the glass that glazes fantasy
has captured your discomfort
and now you think you hear an almost inaudible moan
from a creature that craves dark.

Beware of tripping over the artist's sandalled toes
as you rush to exit.

Mother Goddess
(after the figure in Leeds Art Gallery, artist unknown, Senufo People, Ivory Coast)

My ancestors stretch their canopy of leaves to heaven,
tunnel the African soil with their web of roots.
I carry their DNA in rings of age that spiral my torso.

As a sturdy branch I revelled in the ecstasy
of sap rising. An axe and chisel put an end to that.
I was carved and named Mother Goddess.

My purpose? To initiate boys into men.
I take no credit. My family have always known
the fragility of seeds, the wonders of earth's womb.

Tiny versions of me are carried in men's pockets
but worship is a fickle friend and today you find me
caged in glass for the scrutiny of art lovers –

the antithesis of Eve, rib of Adam.

Gas 1940
(after a painting by Edward Hopper)

All day he had practised his balancing act,
poring over figures, pouring down bourbon.

Now, as New England night falls round him,
he prepares his three scarlet mistresses for sleep.

It is not that he is too old, or refuses to accept
the grime that lodges round his nails;

it is simply that this place, where he feels safe,
is not well travelled and next

he must take down his sign.

Port Vendres – La Ville c.1925
(after a painting by Charles Rennie Mackintosh)

I spotted the title but it could be anywhere.
No skyline. No fishing boats. One yacht hangs
on a deserted quay.

It's more a study of the then white town
with its patchwork of hills as backdrop.
Top right greys hint at the Pyrenees.

That range Didier crossed on foot in 1966
to avoid border checks and two days later
retraced with his Catalan lover

astride a donkey. He'd wooed her in English –
not being a native of the region and she
with only a soupçon of French.

So I'm disappointed in Charles Rennie's painting
with its lack of human figures to suggest
sticky afternoons of passion.

Dancing to forget
(after Slow Swirl at the Edge of the Sea – Mark Rothko, 1944)

As if by chance they touch hands,
dance on sand abandoned by tide.

Swirl in a space cool to toes
edged with pebbles and seaweed trails.

Sky and sea dress in blues
and a yellow sun is gentle

as if it cares ...

a gentle sun is yellow.
Blues dress sea and sky.

Trails of seaweed and pebbles edge toes.
In this cool space they swirl

on tide abandoned sand. Dance,
touch hands, as if by chance,

as if ...

Sea to sky
(after Mark Rothko's painting Green over Blue)

While you have breath
this is the nearest you will get
to the safety of a womb.
Inhale the oily darkness.

Hear the sigh of the tide.

Wipe the damp
from your forehead
and stay in this blue
until salt burns your eyes.

Hear the song of the tide.

The tick-tock of your heart
will start when you take
your plunge

Hear the roar

into whiteness ...

that cloud with fragile edges,
the unreliable promise,
a trick of light.

Part II – Once upon a time

Queen Zenobia

Because my Queen showed me only kindness
and excused me from serving duties
so I might perfect my script,
I feel I must record my truth.

It differs from the myths and lies of powerful men.
Those who give us our history.
But is it not mysterious that no carved image
or coin stamped with Queen Zenobia's face has survived?

There is much to unravel.

My Queen discarded a widow's fate
to raise her dead husband's Kingdom of Palmyra
to dizzy heights. Every caravan travelling the silk road
stopped at her oasis.

Her guests enjoyed good food, fine wines,
soft beds, sweet women and in return were generous.
She received gifts said to rival those sealed
in Tutankhamen's tomb.

And she was sensible with her wealth.
She appointed scholars to teach her favourite son
and invested in fine stallions
for her soldiers.

The truth is, those men with knotted bones
and sagging skin could not usurp the love
of my Queen's people, or prevent her from troubling
the Emperor Aurelian.

The truth is, she did not flee the Emperor's legions
to hide in the marriage bed of a backstreet merchant
whose stew she learnt to cook,
whose house she swept!

The truth is, with her armies, she fought
and to deflect from defeat, Aurelian sought
to woo her.

Servants lose their tongues
when they witness the outrageous
and so I weave my truth in words
furtively scrawled on papyrus.

I was not the girl who filled the royal bath with donkey milk,
nor the child who scented the royal bed
with rose petals,

I was the one assigned to the shadows,
my amphora of wine at the ready should The Roman
have a thirst during his audience with my Queen.

I leave you with what I saw, knowing
you will judge me either honest and loyal
or condemn me for a liar.

Aurelian arrived and found my Queen
in a taunting mood. She boasted of a son,
first-born, best-loved and lodged in a secret place.

Her evasiveness caused The Roman to rage.
He swore his dogs would sniff the child out.
She could expect to receive her boy's head
on a plate.

My Queen faked a swoon,
fell into the Emperor's arms.

Now a Roman's breath is sour, but she lingered
in his embrace, allowed herself to please him,
though she complained
the dagger at his waist was a distraction.

Aurelian unstrapped his weapon,
placed it in my Queen's hands.

What followed is not for the squeamish.

She held his eyes, took his knife and with it
pierced her own slender neck.

I cannot bear to remember her noble blood flooding
that boorish brute of a Roman.

It is my belief that her blood infected him with madness.
Only a mad man could take the eyes and tongues of so many
as he sought to hammer out all traces
of Queen Zenobia's worthy reign.

His hunt for my Queen's son was relentless.
No high-born boy-child was safe from the swords
of his soldiers. But let me assure you,
I deal in facts.

Aurelian was vain.
He had orders to protect the right of Rome
to rule the Kingdom of Palmyra.

If gods were not such fountains of war
I might have fallen on my knobbed knees
and thanked them for a rabid Roman's failure
to notice

this ancient crow sitting in the shade of Palmyrene palms
assisting a lice-ridden boy with his scribblings.

The daughter's story

When I compared my wings
to those you made for my brother,
it was clear you'd skimped on my feathers.

When I told you my wires scratched
and you turned to Icarus with your pot of wax,
I tasted tears.

When you told me I'd be first to leap,
I wet my pants.
Had it not been for your shove …
                                      but the wind is light,
                            my arms don't ache
                                    and you were right,
                            my fear of the sun
                                    was girlish overreaction.

I'm gliding towards a sheltered beach,
        the perfect spot to land and watch.

Sirens

We had no interest in enticing the boozy crew
of that limp-rigged ship onto our rock.

Zeus, the niff of cheesy socks that wafted
ashore on the burps of zephyrs.

Only those with sheep wool stuffed in their ears
could have thought our jeers a song of seduction.

We quickly roused a quarrelling quartet of wind gods
and watched them bully the vessel until, bored,

they set it on course for Ithaca
or some such dreary place.

In the wake of their storming, we spotted a little fellow
strapped to the mast and thought him dead,

though we later learned he was responsible
for phantasmagorical tales

put about to pacify his wife following
an inexcusably long jaunt, with his mates,

to Amsterdam.

On Orchard Street

I summon up a fitter me
from a time when I could swing a shovel.

Together we peel back tarmac, hack
through crops of new build.

A hillside of Victorian terraces
stalls us with its stubborn Yorkshire grit

but soon we reach a path where I straighten
my back to watch my young self

prise up cobbles, dig into soil to release
the steaming smell of horse.

It's thirsty work, and before we leave
we must put everything back to how it was.

But it will be an age before the kids come home,
so let's enjoy swigs of something cool and crisp

and I'll take my forty winks under this Pippin tree
young me has just unearthed.

Conspiracies

Gran said it was a gift and I'd tried to imagine
such a thing wrapped in tissue paper.
Sunday afternoons, while Grandpa snored his boozy doze
the womenfolk drank tea at the kitchen table.

Gran saw our futures in the leaves at the bottom
of each drained cup. Her news was always good;
bingo prizes, handsome strangers and for me
tens in arithmetic.

Once, hushing giggles as they left, the aunts forgot
to mind the door. It banged shut.
Next day me and Gran had an outing to Woolworths.
She bought sunglasses to hide his gift.

She'd seen it coming and said one day I'd understand
why such things are best kept under wraps.

Museum pieces

A hand-sewn pinafore showing skills
of make-do-and-mend. The cover-up
to keep a frock fit for Sunday worship.

Mixing bowl glazed white inside
rich brown outside and big enough
for a week's batch of dough to rise.

Marble kneading slab, black-leaded oven,
a coal scuttle primed to stoke
the smell of baking bread.

Confirmation for our pit lads
that tomorrow's snap would be more
than the paper twist of a mashing.

And what of the misshaped teacake?
Too precious to bin, laced with rogue currants
and christened by our family,

The Raggy Jacket.

Taken straight from the oven and baptized with butter,
we held out our hands to receive a share
as if we were at Sunday Communion.

High tea

Even though we're reduced to two,
Mother has dressed the table in her best Irish linen
and laid our places with bone-handled Sheffield steel,
electroplated napkin rings, the Minton *Indian Tree*.
We thank her God for the egg and potato salad
we are about to receive.

A blueish rim outlines the yolk of my egg wedges
and I think of generations of bright-eyed girls
awash with love; destined to be mothers.
How their horizons were darkened by the pious.
How they were scrubbed of sin.

I pour loose-leaf tea.
Mother waits for me to drain my cup.
She is anxious to perform her pantomime of mystic reading
and declare her daughter's future to be filled with promise.

Moon myths

My mother counsels me as if I'm a stranger
she's met on the bus.

It's unlucky to look at the moon through glass.

I do my best to avoid the ridges and pits
of features treated kindly in nursery books

while my mother, forgetting her own advice,
presses her face to the window.

In thrall to the ruler of springs and neaps,
she feasts on its cheesy sneer.

I turn the silver coin in my pocket,
make my wish,
hear her frail voice insist,

My daughter will be here soon.

Last

He would build up my worn-down heels
to make them last the school year out.

Shoes, he said, were the faces of our souls.
And how he made mine shine, buffing them
with just the right amount of spit,
the right amount of polish.

He had an air of Fred Astaire about him.
I would place my child feet on his toes
and together we'd spin to his favourite 78:
Mantovani's *Moon River*.

He'd trusted me to slot that disc
into its cardboard sleeve
but I abandoned it to a windowsill
where it warped under a hot July sun.

Days later, I skipped to his shed,
searching him out for another pretend dance.
I found him hunched into his disappointment,
at work at his cobbler's last.

Tidy sum
In memory of Dot and Basil

1942
24 hours shore leave for an Able Seaman.
When she asks for time off
the foreman reminds her,
There's a war on.

1943
The Post Office lad on his red bike
corners her street. When he stops
at number 6 there's shame
in her relief.

1957
Never had it so good.
Two weeks in Filey
with candyfloss and fish and chips
twice in one week.

1960
A summer of picnics and when he remembers
to double de-clutch
the third-hand Morris Minor climbs
Sutton Bank like a dream.

1981
Retirement for a man who spent
his working life wearing shoes
that didn't quite fit.

1987
She passes away quietly.
Never one to make a fuss.

1990
He takes a bus
to fill an hour.

1996
He leaves his daughter
£3,000.

Part III – Ghosts

Hauntings

My ghosts do not live in attics, throw china,
or make their strange noises in the night.
They do not congregate in circles on my lawn
or cavort, transparent, before the moon.

My ghosts abandon their grave boxes,
their crematorium urns, to swim the air.
Buoyant as dolphins, they arc the world.
My ghosts are jokers.

One removes keys from my fruit bowl
and places them in the fridge or on the bird feeder.
Another has trained my washing machine
to dissolve one sock from each favourite pair.

Today, a gang of my ghosts greet me in the park.
One sings bird-sweet. Another wafts jasmine.
One babbles a river full of life and dazzles
with a solar eye.

Their talents knock me sideways.
I'm heading for a grazing from gravel
until an inexplicable intervention
keeps me on my feet.

Between 7.30 and 8 a.m.

Snow veils a waking sky,
drapes young shoots in bridal wear.
A brief visit in a rushing year.
It is melting as she stirs a tear into
her chipped breakfast cup:
a present from Blackpool – circa 1938.

Shed

These walls are drunk on turps and tobacco.
Shelves sag with tins of dried-up gloss
and part-used cans of silk and matt
in shades that are my childhood.

Horsehair brushes, stuffed in jars,
have supped their ration of white spirit
and the smell – think Old Spice
with undertones of dubbin wax.

Bought from the widow of a para,
an oak blanket box squats by the door.
The grain is lost to layers of polish.
Mother wouldn't have it in the house.

So his ashtray sits on its lid,
cradling a mound of Silk Cut stubs,
doubling as a paperweight for his note
back in 5 nipped to pub.

These foolish things

Your song pays homage
to cigarettes with lipstick traces
on evenings a stranger insists,
It's cold outside.

In my head your improvisation
revolves like a 78.

We are in the kitchen.
You peel potatoes, eyes screwed
against smoke curls from the cigarette
clasped between your lips.
A medley of romance escapes
from the side of your mouth
and I'm fascinated
by how your Woodbine transforms
to an art form of ash
before scattering.

They say I'll miss you less
as time goes by.

Navigating St George's Channel

Dusk, like a bad lad, menaces my deck.
I change the jib, reef the main,
curse waterproofs for liars.

      Mean moon, foul wind, salt spray
           throw doubts on my plotted course;
                my dancing compass heading.

I have no god to blame for emptying the sea
of port and starboard company
as night thickens, yet in answer

      to an un-prayed prayer, the Dog Star shines down;
         illuminates my mother,
            in Sunday hat.

She's dry as ash I scattered and cannot blink away.
She holds me calm, takes me back
to walk on Bridlington beach and I know

      this is the year I learned to swim.
        She buttons my cardigan,
           tucks up my skirt, leaves me
               to paddle.

In a surging tide I topple through the eye of my storm
to land on a steady deck where a storm jib flaps
in a muddy dawn.

The art of frying eggs

I know before I prod my fork into the egg
it's overcooked. Not a drip of yolk
and I hear you, in the crackle of hot fat,
asking,

What is it with you and eggs?

And I'm telling you
to make your own flaming breakfast
and reminding you of what the doctor said
about fried food, heart disease and stroke.

I study the fork, its four prongs:

> those corny chat-up lines you fed me,
> the vows we made, for better or worse,
> our storm-proof nest, or so we thought,
> me, in this kitchen, frying one egg.

In dreams I cook the perfect sunny side up
and feel the warmth of your lips brush my neck.

Part IV – Shades of childhood

Impact

If it had been an asteroid
on a spin towards our world
a team of NASA scientists
would have given warning.

There was none of that.
It wasn't even Sunday.
Daddy was at work and Mammy
up to her elbows in pie-pastry.

We kids played in the street.
Our Billy, in to bat, was squinting at the sun.
He didn't duck.
It was the dullest thud.

Guardian

I'm so light I could skip on this river
and not cause a ripple.

A ferry will come –
here is your coin for the man at the tiller.

Is that Granny, on the opposite bank?
Is she laying out a picnic?

Steady when you step aboard –
don't giggle.

Will there be fish fingers and chunky chips?
Can I play games on my tablet?

When you give your coin to the man
look only at his feet.

Who will check on Mummy and Daddy?
Will they remember to feed my fish?

When you step off the ferry
do not look back.

Here comes the boat.
I think it's a little early.

We all do my dove.

Will you come with me?

I've come as far as I'm allowed.

Will I see you again?

For sure.

Being but kids
(a response to Being But Men by Dylan Thomas)

Being but kids, we run into the trees
to spook baddies with spells and chants.
Rooted, beneath an ancient oak,
we look up
to where feathered devils roost.

We have not come as bad boys
to steal eggs, bait snares and be off
with a sack of last night's catch
for Sunday's oven.
We're here for magic.

It's late when we brave the climb
to pierce a leafy roof and find the moon,
pale as Dracula's bride, in a rain of stars.

Grown-ups might pen poems
to such lunar weirdness and not wish
for mothers, warm beds and Horlicks,

but we're kids. We run into trees.

Arguments

At cousin Joe's
we leave grown-ups
to natter in the kitchen.
We sneak to the front room
to play *Driving the Bus.*
Joe says, *Only lads drive buses.*
I pull his hair.
I make him cry.
To stop his whine
I let him sit on an arm
of the giant settee
and pretend to steer me,
my doll and his panda
to a town called Seaside.
Joe shouts, *We've arrived.*
Dad storms in,
throws me my blazer.
We leave without my doll
and I'm running to keep up.
I don't think Dad's talking to me
when he blurts, *I'm done
with that brother of mine.*

Fifty years on Dad's heart gives out.
I check his address book.
I put a notice in the paper.
I go in search of a house I remember
and find a slip road leading to the A65.

Shrove Tuesday
(traditionally a day for children to play with a whip and top)

You were three when you learnt to squint stars,
turn them into dancing tutus with nods of your head
and demand everyone in the house shout

> *I believe in fairies.*

At five you hopscotched the garden path
to your mother's vegetable patch and failed to find
that pea-green boat.

Aged seven your present was a spinning top
you chalked with a rainbow, spun with your hands
until it bled a riot of colour.

You whispered,
> *My father keeps a whip*

and you blew on your palms.

Prey

He took flight when the sky darkened.
His voice had not yet deepened.
There's no trace of his journey to your home
with its garden brocade of marigolds and daisies.

Stunned by your roses,
the way they flaunt on your fence,
pulse with perfume,
he ignored frenzied clouds of bees,
the clumps of stinging nettles.

I watched you open your gate,
guide him down your path,
lead him through your door.
God forgive me.

Part V – Spotlight

sixties usherette

i aimed my spotlight on back-row lovers
left a scattering of butterkist in the projectionists box
turned up the heat during lawrence of arabia
to boost sales of lyonsmaids and vanilla tubs

i let shoeless kids in through a fire escape
for an afternoon with mary poppins
and each night
before going to my bed
i stood on a copy of sporting pink
to shake out my frock

i had no time for that board of film censors
i let 14-year-olds watch butterfield 8
because someone had told me
it would be three more years
before sex began for the british

i know where i was when jfk took his bullets —
upper circle ladies checking toilet paper stocks
a woman smelling of fish and chips
told me what she'd heard
on the bbc home service

i worked seven nights a week and matinees
and it was a sacking offence to have
a row of seats untipped
when the recording of god save the queen
played its last note.

Last words

Eunice,
I'm taking a
bath. Leave out
bourbon and
my Chanel.
Forget the
sleeping tablets.
I'm expecting a call
from *You Know Who*.
He worries. People talk.
He scolded me for my
performance on his
birthday and I told
him he was a silly
boy. Remember
to leave my red
shoes and mink
cape handy. He
may send his
limousine for
me. Go now
and put up
your feet.

Eunice Murray was Marilyn Monroe's last housekeeper.

We all have the makings of a star

Because everybody loves a clown
I put myself centre stage,
in baggy pants, a whitened face,
mascara eyes, lipstick mouth,
Chaplin's too-small bowler.
I pluck a carnation from my sleeve,
offer it to you,
but the god of cock-ups
snaps off the blooming head.
I wince at slow handclaps.
It isn't all bad.
The stagehands split their sides;
roll out a cannon from the wings,
powder primed for my blast
into fame's dark matter.

Look me up in a millennium or two.

For the record

He said she looked too innocent.
He could not capture his perfect shot.
I noticed only how she shivered.

From my bag of tricks I took Kohl
to outline her eyes. Did you see the photo
in the 1957 National Portrait Exhibition?

Those were the days when everyone
wanted a piece of her and some would say
I carved her up. No.

I was her trusted aide and conjured auburn curls
from next to nothing. Everywhere she went
my blend of sandalwood and jasmine lingered.

When I couldn't contain the signs of age
and her wealth had been snatched by bailiffs,
we shared my small flat in Greenwich.

I earned a modest living
holding an occasional séance.
She did not want for wine or cigarettes.

The day she failed to appear at breakfast
I found her in bed, bare-faced and wigless.
I worked my magic.

I shut her eyes, applied the make-up
and crowned her
with a mass of tight tonged curls.

The papers got it wrong.

I'll grant she died without a penny,
but since that freezing day
she'd been loved.

It's lunchtime and I've been reading Frank O'Hara

I go for a walk in my town,
which is not laid out on the grid system,
like New York or Milton Keynes.
Here, roads skirt the curves of ancient boundaries.
There are schoolkids, queueing in Greggs
for slices of pizza, packets of crisps and drinks
in primary colours.
Builders chat and wait for pork pies to be released
from the oven.
An office worker cycles past.
He's searching for a café that understands vegan needs.
Rain is in the air.

I walk to the river hoping to see a kingfisher.
I spot a pair of adolescents *making whoopee.*
My mother would use that phrase even though
she'd never been to New York or Milton Keynes.
They're not the right words for this pair with their hunger
no meal-deal will fix.

On the opposite side of the river an Italian restaurant
has opened and I think you'd like it, Frank.
It's been sympathetically converted from a mill
where families of townsfolk once worked.
I've booked a table there for Sunday. A treat
for the family. I might have sardines, although sardines
can be a problem when you're so far from the sea.
I wonder if Alan Bennett likes Italian cuisine.
I once saw him, in Bettys, having afternoon tea.

If my lot were given a sandwich and slice of Victoria sponge, they'd have to stop off at the chippy on their way home.

No offence Frank, but it's time I moved on
to spend the remains of the day with Dr John Cooper Clarke
and Wendy Cope.

Part VI – Some you lose

Pre-nuptial

We agreed not to tell of our meeting on the stairs
twelve hours before your wedding.

You reeked of risk, said I smelled of Sunday-school soap
and tasted like a Bacchanalia

and what we did, for old times' sake,
meant everything meant nothing.

The pressure of your thumbs left blooms on my arms;
stains that don't scrub out.

Note to silence

After the neighbours moved
taking their arguments and howling dogs
you made brief visits and I treasured our moments
before the kids arrived home.

When my eldest moved to student digs
and the young one took off with an Interrail ticket,
you began to encroach, so I flirted
with early morning radio and The Archers.

Like a crêpe-soled stalker you pursued me;
ignored my need for the din of the living.
This is just to let you know I'll be spending my nights
tuned to World Service.

This is just to say
(with apologies to William Carlos Williams)

I have used your
toupee
to clean your
Mercedes.

It gave
a brilliant shine
but now
it's quite limp.

Please,
have my chamois,
if you think
it will help.

Blues Café

At a table for two in Blues Café
she ekes out the dregs of chamomile tea
watches rain streak winter-dark windows
car lights illuminate cycle lane seas.
Rolls back her dress cuff, checks on her wristwatch,
smiles at the waitress who's ready for home,
gets to her feet, it's time she was leaving;
who would have guessed she'd still be on her own?

Then the door opens. Is this a punter?
Will the game start? Will his money flow free?
She cuts the small talk; straight to business
tells him the extras and tots up his fee.

Next day Blues Café's an incident scene.
She's first-class on Virgin living her dream.

Saying it with flowers

My best friend came with daffodils,
work sent a mixed bouquet,
neighbours arrived with a potted plant
after my hospital stay.

The kids are looking after me,
take turns to change my socks.
Lucy's little school friends gave me pansies
tucked in a painted egg box.

And when you're free to visit
I know you'll want to be
clear about your feelings, how much
you care for me.

I picture you so clearly
striding that shopping aisle;
picking the prettiest checkout girl,
flashing your even-toothed smile.

You'll bluster in with roses,
no time to stop for tea.
When you've gone I'll find the label:
Buy One – Get One Free!

Dandelion

Hey Dandy – aren't you the cheeky one
snuggled in bed with those hybrids.

It's a puzzle where you get your looks
when, as a bud, you're not promising;
eagerly embrace the punk craze
with your spikey head.

But look at you today, flashy as the sun,
tap root anchored.

I've seen your brothers on the lawn,
laying low with pink-tipped daisies,
and your cousins on the river bank,
under the blackberry's bush

sniffing garlic, dreaming of brew-ups
with burdock.

And all of you addicted to the bees;
need to honey them over and over
until you go seedy, grow weedy,
like some stubbed cigarette.

Gathered round the oak, frail elders wait,
and here's the rub –

your sort breeze along on a child's puff.

Dreams

Sometimes I dream I've been reincarnated
with long legs, and knees free from arthritis
or I'm the guest on Desert Island Discs
granted my wish to take Nancy Sinatra's
These Boots Are Made for Walkin'
as the must-have single along with
The Tripitaka in place of The Bible,
The Complete Works of Shakespeare,
in extra-large print, and my luxury item,
you've guessed: long legs, because I'd like to take
one stride instead of three in order to keep
up with you but best of all I'd discover
an inch of clearance between my crotch and every
five-bar gate where you left me – perched.

Swan song

It's a breath-stealing climb he takes in his stride
as he chats about plans for another motorbike trip.

I gasp for air, think of coffee, until the birds pipe up
with a serenade like no other. A love song

that makes the sun laser clouds and our little lives
nothing but a chime of semi-quavers in a sonata.

Human voices intrude, mute the birds.
The walkers bustle past bagging their miles.

He takes my hand and tells me he's decided against
Route du Soleil in favour of the RN7.

Today, I'm alone on a path with no incline
trying to ignore alarm calls from blackbirds.

Dance of doves at Lanzarote

On the road to Manrique's House
the sea is a reflection of sky's pristine blue.
The sun stares down
and nothing dare intrude on this backdrop
for a flock of paloma blanca
as they rise in synchronized flight
to catch the light and shape-shift –
a shoal of fish in a waltz
across our scrap of heaven.

In the late artist's home, a choreography
I believed too difficult to interpret in oils
hangs on the wall; a testament to enchantment
or the dazzle that distracted the day
he failed to notice an oncoming car.

The mistress

I'm done with lies and have retired
to become a yacht, broad of beam
with long keel. I'm built for an easy ride.
Fitted with a reliable outboard
I propel through the doldrums on autopilot
then run before the wind with my sails goose-winged
on a course across the horizon
to where I find his old sloop moored
beneath Orion's belt. I tie alongside. Wait
for him to down warm beer and spin a yarn
to his once pretty wife about tidal range
and the need to check lines.
When his naked soles explore my oiled teak deck
zephyrs sing sweet nothings from my rigging.

Part VII – To be continued

Leaving Palmyra – March 2011

At The Pancake House
we drank pomegranate juice and sang

Midnight at the Oasis.

A man with a golden grin and box of oils
moved between tables.

He offered free head massages.
The tabbouleh arrived to save us.

The man told us to visit the ruins at sunrise
before wind whipped up sand.

We took his advice but soon our horizon
was lost to advancing dust clouds.

We rushed back to the café.

Our friend with the precious smile had waited
to deliver us to Damascus.

We scrambled into his jeep. The smoke
from burnt pancakes seared our throats.

Sand beat on the canvas hood
as we jolted along desert roads.

Goodbyes at the airport were hurried.

In Starbucks on St Paul's Street we order flat whites.
We've nothing to sing about.

Adrift

and sirens consider us unworthy
        of attention.
Our lives have unravelled
        like badly coiled rope.
Being too many
        for this toytown boat
we cradle our children.

        Someone shouts,

                Hold on

as we rise,
        then

            f
           a
           l
            l

        on the sickening swell.

The engine takes a soaking.
        Sky signals its red warning.

Mayday

The hiccup in your health left you with a disregard for safety.
We should have turned left after crossing the bridge
but you are not about to let a guidebook dictate.

> It's hot and I'm not dressed for this.
> My legs are a Miro of scratches;
> shoulders scorched,
> feet blistered.

We find ourselves on the edge of a cliff looking down
at a sea so calm, so blue that when you offer me
your hand I think, yes, we could tumble
through air, make our big splash,
if only I was as ready as you,
for such a finale.

> I turn from the pull of the drop.
> Salt stings my cheeks, my lips.
> I limp to the bridge, follow
> the prescribed path.

You never again tempt me with a reckless act
and when I get the call, from a foreign port,
there's no need for a translation.

Fighter

She fills conscious moments
with uphill feats;
counts the thuds of her feet
and never questions
how her damaged heart can race.
When her body craves respite
she recites tenses of the verb *to be*.
Her brain is dull.
She flushes medication down the loo
and with it the technicolour magician
who invaded her nights, sawed her in two,
and made off
with her other half.
Now sleep is dreamless.
Morning rings alarm.
She reacts to bells – seconds out.
No loitering in a king-sized bed
for fear of rolling over,
coming face to face with space.

Invisible injuries

Respecting her privacy we didn't intrude but took turns
to check the rhythm of her curtains.
My mistake was to offer a cake dusted with icing sugar.
She knocked it to the floor; shut me out.
To save face I disengaged
but Graham from the cul-de-sac
stuck two fingers up to threats of prosecution.
He broke in through her kitchen window
called the ambulance.
She came home today loaded with prescriptions
but those of us who understand the deviousness of demons
continue to monitor the rhythm of her curtains.

Some say

you're an unbalanced wheel
a poorly thrown pot
need a corset
to strengthen your core
an iron to smooth and straighten
your back
a key to unlock your door

I say

you're an orb of blown glass
a fine filament
wired to switch on my sun
and you glow with the shine
of a new pair of shoes
that know
they were made to run

Good dog

Mornings,
I walk your dog in the park.
She chases a ball,
brings it back,
drops it at my feet.
I believe she accepts me
as pack leader.
I do not put down
her loss of appetite to grief until
the new owner of your Harley
is stopped by temporary traffic lights
on our street.

Your dog's ears prick to attention
at that particular sound a Fat Boy makes
with its engine ticking over.
I watch as she heads for the gate,
her tail a blur of wags.
Red turns green.
A belch of exhaust muffles her bark.

Through the sting in my eyes I see your dog turn.
She is coming to sit at my left heel.

On my last trip

I head for a southern port where heat treats
swollen joints kindly. At the harbour café
I down a coffee laced with brandy while finalizing
the purchase of a boat I can navigate singlehanded.

The day is cloudless of course.

I sail to the line between sea and sky to find the place
you've anchored. I tie alongside – swim ashore
to the bar where you drink cold beer
with dark-eyed glossy women.

You look up when I walk in, hold out your arms
inviting me into the safest of harbours.
I shake my head and laugh when you ask
Where the hell have you been?

The next Big Bang

Because we are destined to turn to dust
I have committed you to memory.

When I miss you the most it is your hands that haunt me
with their square scrubbed nails.

I am surrounded by your handiwork from cellar to loft,
garden to garage.

I sit on the chaise you re-covered and tot up
the broken things you saved.

I lie on the bed you made and I hear stars being born.
I am expectant with thoughts

of thunderous applause greeting the instant
a speck of you and a fleck of me collide.